The Seat Belt Song

Story by Jenny Giles
Illustrations by Rachel Tonkin

"The police have come to school today
to talk to us about seat belts,"
said Miss Bell.
"It's time to go out and meet them."

"I'm going to be a police officer
when I grow up," said Andrew.
"And I'm going to be
a police officer, too,"
said Zoe, as they walked to the door.

3

When the children were all
sitting down outside,
the police officer said,
"Good morning, children.
I'm Officer Williams,
and this is Officer Young.
We would like you to sing
The Seat Belt Song with us."

4

Officer Young held up a big card.
It said:

The Seat Belt Song

(Tune: *Twinkle Twinkle Little Star*)

We can sing the seat belt song,
Join with us and sing along.
Find the seat belt,
Pull it down,
Hold it tightly,
Put it around.
We all know this safety trick.
Do it up, and make it
CLICK!

The children sang with the officers.

"That's a great song!" said Andrew.
"Can we sing it again?"

Officer Williams smiled.
"Soon," he said, "but now
you are all going to practice
putting on a seat belt."

"You must **always** remember
to put your seat belt on
as soon as you get into a car,"
said Officer Young.

The Seat Belt Song
(Tune: *Twinkle Twinkle Little Star*)

We can sing the seat belt song,
Join with us and sing along.
Find the seat belt,
Pull it down,
Hold it tightly,
Put it around.
We all know this safety trick.
Do it up, and make it
CLICK!

The children got into
the police car, four at a time.

The officers watched carefully
as the children put their seat belts on.
Click! Click! Click! Click!
Everyone had a turn.

"Well done, everyone!"
said Officer Williams,
and then he looked at Andrew.
"Would you like to sing to us now?"
he asked.
"Then you can get into the car
and turn on the siren."

Andrew ran up to the car.
Officer Williams took off his police hat
and put it on Andrew's head.

Andrew sang *The Seat Belt Song*,
and everyone cheered.
Then he climbed into the car
and turned on the siren.

The light on top of the car
flashed around and around,
and the siren screamed out
across the playground.

"Turn it off!" shouted the children.
Andrew turned the siren off
and jumped out of the car.

"We need a new person now,"
said Officer Young.

"Zoe wants to be a police officer!"
said Andrew.

But Zoe looked down at the ground.
"I'm not very good at singing,"
she said.

The Seat Belt
(Tune :Twinkle twinkl)

We can sing the seat belt
Join with us and sing along
Find the seat belt,
Pull it down,
Hold it tightly,
Put it round.
We all know this safety trick
Do it up and make it
CLICK!

"I'll help you," said Andrew.
"Come on!"

Zoe got up slowly.
Officer Young put her police hat
on Zoe's head,
and Andrew and Zoe
sang the song together.

Then Zoe got into
the police car
and pulled the seat belt down.
"Well done, Zoe!" said Officer Young.

"Oh, no!" cried Andrew.
"I forgot!"

Andrew watched as Zoe
turned the siren on
and then off again.
"I forgot to put on my seat belt!
I wasn't a very good police officer,"
he said.

"Oh, yes you were," said Officer Young,
"because you helped Zoe.
Helping people is a very
important part of our job, too.
So you **both** did very well."

"I won't **ever** forget my seat belt
again," said Andrew,
as he and Zoe gave the hats back
to the police officers.

The children all waved goodbye
to the police officers.
Then they walked back
to their classroom singing:

We can sing the seat belt song,
Join with us and sing along.
Find the seat belt,
Pull it down,
Hold it tightly,
Put it around.
We all know this safety trick.
Do it up, and make it
CLICK!